Can I tell you about Epilepsy?

Can I tell you about...?

The 'Can I tell you about...?' series offers simple introductions to a range of limiting conditions. Friendly characters invite readers to learn about their experiences of living with a particular condition and how they would like to be helped and supported. These books serve as excellent starting points for family and classroom discussions.

other books in the Can I tell you about...? series

Can I tell you about Asperger Syndrome?
A guide for friends and family
Jude Welton
Foreword by Elizabeth Newson
Illustrated by Jane Telford
ISBN 978 1 84310 206 9
eISBN 978 1 84642 422 9

Can I tell you about Selective Mutism?
A guide for friends, family and professionals
Maggie Johnson and Alison Wintgens
Illustrated by Robyn Gallow
ISBN 978 1 84905 289 4
eISBN 978 0 85700 611 0

of related interest

Children with Seizures
A Guide for Parents, Teachers, and Other Professionals
Martin L. Kutscher MD
Foreword by Gregory L. Holmes MD
ISBN 978 1 84310 823 8
eISBN 978 1 84642 490 8
Part of the JKP Essentials series

Can I tell you about Epilepsy?

A guide for friends, family and professionals

KATE LAMBERT

Illustrated by Scott Hellier

Jessica Kingsley *Publishers*
London and Philadelphia

First published in 2012
by Jessica Kingsley Publishers
116 Pentonville Road
London N1 9JB, UK
and
400 Market Street, Suite 400
Philadelphia, PA 19106, USA

www.jkp.com

Library of Congress Cataloging in Publication Data
Lambert, Kate.
Can I tell you about epilepsy? : a guide for friends, family, and
professionals / Kate Lambert ; illustrated
by Scott Hellier.
p. cm.
Includes bibliographical references.
ISBN 978-1-84905-309-9 (alk. paper)
1. Epilepsy in children–Juvenile literature. I. Title.
RJ496.E6L36 2012
618.92'853–dc23
2012005064

British Library Cataloguing in Publication Data
A CIP catalogue record for this book is available from the British Library

ISBN 978 1 84905 309 9
eISBN 978 0 85700 648 6

Printed and bound in Great Britain

To my wonderful daughter, Lille. You are a bundle
of love and light and a superb representative
for someone living with Absence Seizures.
And to my mum, Gina, without whose wisdom,
unfaltering support and subtle guidance I may not
have had the strength to make the right choices
for Lille in those early days following diagnosis.

Acknowledgements

I would like to thank Lesley Pierce whose passion for a more healthy way of life has inspired the choices I have made for Lille. Victoria Flinders whose emails and information in the early days pointed a gentle finger in the right direction. My family, my loyal band of brothers, and my wonderful friends, the "Fly girls" – none of you have ever doubted me and you surround Lille and I with love. The parents on Facebook who are part of the group "Parents of children with Absence Seizures" – you are dotted all over the world but being able to talk to others in my shoes has meant I have never felt alone. Scott Hellier for his wonderful and creative illustrations. JKP for allowing me this opportunity.

But most of all to Gina Lambert who held my hand tightly through the hard times. I hope I can be as loyal and as supportive a mum.

And to my lovely, unique, creative, funny, warm-hearted "Lillepad" for being truly amazing and for inspiring this book.

Contents

Author note

The characters in this book represent three of the common forms of Epilepsy and the ways in which it can present itself. Epilepsy is a complex condition, and while it is hoped that the reader is able to identify with and make connections with the experiences of the characters herein, the author acknowledges that each case of Epilepsy is unique to the individual and arrives with its own set of Epilepsy circumstances.

Introduction

This book has been written to help everyone understand Epilepsy and its varying forms. It is written from the perspective of children with Epilepsy.

- Children with an epileptic condition are able to indentify with the young characters in the book who represent various different forms of Epilepsy.

- Family, friends and professionals can read from a child's perspective what Epilepsy feels like, what it can look like and how they can help.

- It is a useful, simply written and friendly book to share with children who have Epilepsy, designed to be used as a conversation starter in talking about Epilepsy and how it affects them.

- Extra sections at the back give tips for teachers and parents to help support children with Epilepsy in important areas such as their education.

- The book includes clear descriptions of what Epilepsy is and what happens in the brain and describes the different kinds of epilepsy, including Absence Seizures, Focal (Partial) Seizures and Tonic Clonic Seizures. It also includes important first-aid procedures for seizures.

"There are many different kinds of Epilepsy. I'd like to tell you about mine. Allow me to introduce you to my friends, Charlie and Ahmed, who also have Epilepsy. They will tell you about theirs too. Knowing more about Epilepsy will mean that, if you'd like to, you can help."

"Everyone with Epilepsy has their own unique experiences. My friends and I all describe our own kind of Epilepsy.

On the outside we look like everybody else. We act like everybody else too. I like to do things just like other girls my age – I like dancing, swimming and reading. Charlie likes riding his bike and Ahmed loves painting. You wouldn't be able to tell we have Epilepsy unless you saw us have a seizure.

We will tell you what it feels like to have Epilepsy and what may happen if we have a seizure. The kinds of seizures my friends and I talk to you about are different because we have different kinds of Epilepsy."

"Epilepsy simply describes when there is a sudden change in how our brains work – this can cause a change to our movements or actions for a little while. These changes are called a seizure. Epilepsy is not a disease that you can catch, like a cold or measles.

I think it is important that you know what a seizure looks like. Many people think a seizure is when you fall on the floor and your body shakes, but that is just one kind. In this book you will hear about some different kinds of seizures.

A seizure happens to me when a sudden change in my brain sends confusing messages to my body, which my body doesn't understand. Depending on what part of the brain the message was sent from, it can have a different effect on the body.

Mine, Charlie's and Ahmed's all start in different areas of our brains and that is why our seizures are different."

"Let's start with me. I have Absence Seizures. When I have a seizure, I stare blankly, blink or wander around without realising. I may look as though I am ignoring you but I am actually having a seizure. Sometimes I might make some movements with my lips or 'get stuck' in the last action I was making. Let's say I was colouring in. I might continue with the action of colouring in while having a seizure but not know that I was doing it.

This makes my kind of seizure tricky to spot as people may think I'm just daydreaming. When someone is daydreaming, you can usually get their attention by saying their name. When I am having a seizure, I will not be able to hear you and can't be brought around until my seizure has ended. This may only be seconds but often I can have hundreds of these a day. If I do have lots of seizures, they can often make me feel very tired and sometimes I may not feel like playing sports or games in the playground."

"I may need information repeated
if I have missed something
while having a seizure."

"Because of my seizures, I sometimes miss bits of what people are saying, like when I am listening to my teacher in class. It can sometimes make me feel embarrassed or confused because I don't know the answer or because I am not clear about what is going on around me.

Having an Absence Seizure is as if my brain is a movie that has been paused, but for everyone else the movie is carrying on. I may not hear information or chunks of conversation, or I may hear the beginning of an instruction but perhaps not the end.

For example, if someone said 'You can come in the house, but you must take off your shoes', I might hear 'you can come in the house' but not the instruction to 'take off your shoes'.

If I didn't take my shoes off, this might be seen as me being naughty or rude, when in actual fact I hadn't heard this part of the instruction. It would really help me if you would check that I have heard everything that has been said."

"Even when I'm not having a seizure, there may still be Epilepsy-type 'waves' happening in my brain, or I may have had seizures during the night time. Both can make me feel distracted, tired or restless, or may make me behave in a way I don't want to."

"It is not always easy to see that it might be my Epilepsy that causes me to behave in ways that I don't want to. When my parents, teachers or friends get annoyed or frustrated with me, it can make me feel misunderstood.

It would really help me if people understood that the way I behave is not always something I can help. A bit of patience and understanding from the people around me would make things much easier for me.

If I need a rest or some time out during the day, please understand this. A soft, quiet corner of the classroom or at home would be a great resting place for me. If I wanted company, a caring friend to stay with me would be even better!"

"I have Focal Seizures. This is
where my seizure will feel or look
different depending on which
part of my brain is affected."

"My seizures can happen differently each time I have them. Sometimes I may be awake and aware of what is happening but unable to control what my body is doing. At other times I may be unconscious while the seizure is happening and so I may feel a bit confused afterwards.

Our brains are very clever at telling us how things taste, smell, look and sound. When I have a seizure, my brain changes suddenly and sends me mixed-up messages. It can make things look bigger or smaller than they are, and it can also affect my hearing or make me smell or taste something that is not real. This is called a *hallucination*. This might sound strange to you, but if people around me know that this is what happens, they can reassure me about what is real and what is not."

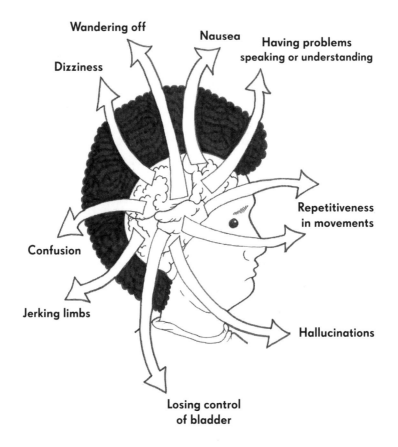

Wandering off

Nausea

Having problems
speaking or understanding

Dizziness

Repetitiveness
in movements

Confusion

Jerking limbs

Hallucinations

Losing control
of bladder

"Focal Seizures can be different for everyone. These are some of the things you might see when someone has a Focal Seizure, depending on which part of their brain is affected."

"I might have a different kind of seizure which affects just one part of my body; for example, my right arm might jerk. This may look strange to you, but it is my brain giving my body those mixed-up messages. Just because my actions look deliberate, please don't think I am in control of them.

If you know what is happening to me, then perhaps you won't stare or laugh or say anything that might make me feel bad. These things can make me feel very sad or embarrassed. It would really help me if I knew my seizures were understood by the people around me.

It would also help if you are aware that during Focal Seizures sometimes the mixed-up messages can 'march' to other areas of my brain and so my seizure could progress to a different kind. Please stay with me until I am fully recovered and aware of my surroundings.

Like other seizures, mine can make me feel tired or confused. It would help me if I had somewhere soft and quiet to rest, and if I wanted company, a caring friend to sit with me would be even better!"

"I have Tonic Clonic Seizures. This is where I lose consciousness and fall to the floor and my body jerks."

"Tonic Clonic Seizures are the kind most people recognise and the most common form of Epilepsy.

Tonic is the name given to the part of the seizure where I fall to the floor. My body goes stiff because my muscles are tightening, a bit like when we stretch in gym class – the difference is I'm not in control of this.

Clonic is the part where my arms and legs start to jerk because my muscles are relaxing and tightening quickly. You may notice a blue colour around my mouth. This is because my breathing is irregular.

Having a seizure like this is as exhausting as running a marathon! So I may not feel or behave like myself afterwards. I may need to sleep to allow my body and brain time to recover.

Having Tonic Clonic Seizures can sometimes mean that I lose control of my bladder. I have no control over this. It would really help me if you would cover me up with a blanket or coat to save me being embarrassed."

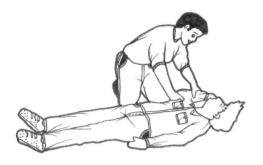

"This is how to put someone into the recovery position. It would help me if you could put me into this position once my seizure has ended."

"My seizure can't be stopped and it would be harmful to me if you tried, but there are some vital things you can do if you are around me when I have a sezure. It may help me if you learnt some basic first aid.

When I have a seizure:

- Please protect me by removing any dangerous objects that might be nearby.

- Please don't try to hold me still or try to move me unless I am near danger.

- Please don't try to 'wake me' or put anything in my mouth.

- Cushion my head with something soft.

- Look to see if I have an Epilepsy identity card.

- Call for an ambulance if I need medical attention or if my seizure lasts for more than five minutes.

- Gently move me into the recovery position shown in the pictures on page 26.

- When my seizure has finished, please stay with me and help me by being calm. I shouldn't be given anything to eat or drink until I am feeling better."

"Please don't feel afraid of my
Epilepsy. My seizures may look scary,
but I hope that now you understand
them you may feel less afraid. It would
help me if you remembered that,
apart from the brief moments when
I have a seizure, I am just like you."

"Medicine that has such a big job to do is very powerful and so can have some side effects."

"Everyone with Epilepsy has different ways of controlling their seizures. You might know someone with Epilepsy but be unaware that they have it. Seizures can be completely managed through medication. For others, they may take medication but may still have seizures which 'break through'.

Sometimes medication doesn't work or the person with Epilepsy chooses not to take it because of the side effects. In some cases, surgery may be possible if medication doesn't work.

Others choose a natural route, without prescribed medication, to help manage their seizures. This might mean the person is on a special diet. It would help if you understood why they have to eat certain things and not others.

Many of us take medication and so it would help if you understood the effects it can have. We can tell you how our medication affects us personally if you ask."

"Let's learn to accept the things that make us unique and help each other with our difficulties. It would help make our world a safe and happy place to be."

"The majority of us with Epilepsy have learnt to accept our condition and manage ourselves very well.

One of the biggest problems we face is the way other people react. Because people sometimes don't understand what is happening during a seizure, it can seem scary or strange. This can lead to people being unkind, which can hurt.

Please remember that there are things that make me similar to you and things that make me different. We all have things that make us different from each other. If we didn't, the world would be a very boring place!

My name is Charlie. I like riding my bike, climbing and writing stories. I also have Epilepsy. It's just a part of me which makes me unique."

How teachers can help

"Epilepsy is a variable disorder and it will affect us in different ways. Some of us may, at times, experience learning or behavioural problems. The impact of my Epilepsy must be considered according to my own individual experience."

LEARNING AND ORGANISATION

"It is important that my teacher understands that the medication I take can have side effects. Medication can have different effects on people with Epilepsy so it is important that the class teacher knows it can affect my behaviour.

Many medications for Epilepsy can affect memory and so I can sometimes have difficulty remembering data and information. The seizures themselves can affect energy levels and focus, so un-medicated children may need extra help with organisation and self-management too. There are ways you can help with this:

- It may help me if information and tasks are broken down into small, manageable chunks. For instance, reading a paragraph, stopping and asking me questions about what I have read before continuing may help me to digest new information.

- Having a checklist in my desk or tray could help me with my organisation. My checklist could include a schedule of the day's events or reminders of what I need to bring home from school, like my instrument, homework or lunch bag. It could also have a section which can be pulled out and taken home to remind me what I need to remember to bring back to school for the next day. My teacher could encourage me to check my list at the end of the school day.

- To help with memory, older children may like to write reminder notes to themselves or may benefit from recording the content of an important class using a dictaphone, for example.

- Extra time in tests may help with my ability to recall information.

- It is easy to assume that the more subtle forms of Epilepsy have less impact on my learning. Absence Seizures can affect my learning if they are under-acknowledged. This is because the seizures can cause gaps in what I hear. If a question is presented to me verbally, for example 'What is 2 + 2 + 4?', I may hear 'What is 2 + 2 blank?' and I may think that the answer is 4 instead of 8. If I am told my answer is wrong, this may lead to confusion and lack of confidence surrounding my learning. Visuals to support the questioning, such as formula or number cards, may help me. It is less likely that I will miss information that will still be visible when my seizure has ended.

- It would really help me if I was seated close to the teacher so that things can be repeated if needed without making me stand out too much. Sometimes I feel too embarrassed to say the things I have missed because I want to avoid giving attention to my seizures. Subtle questioning may help to decipher my understanding. As well as this, my teacher will have a better chance of spotting a seizure if I am seated nearby."

UNDERSTANDING CHANGES

- "Epilepsy sufferers can vary in how they are feeling – there may be good weeks when the seizures are low and there may bad weeks when the seizures are high. Having a soft, quiet area of the classroom where I know I can go if I need to rest or sleep after a seizure would be very reassuring for me. A caring friend would help me to avoid feeling isolated.

- Teachers must take all forms of Epilepsy seriously, no matter how frequent or infrequent the seizures are. My seizures may be well controlled, but please be aware that during growth spurts, times of stress or adjustments in medication, I may have a breakthrough. My teacher may misunderstand my change in behaviour or my lack of motivation, and this can cause me frustration. The support and understanding of my teacher is vital for me."

COMMUNICATING WITH OTHERS

- "A communication book between my parents/carers and my teacher is vital to ensure that both those at school and those at home are aware of how I am doing. It is important that my teacher works closely with my parents/carers who may be very 'in tune' with my seizures. They may be able to tell you my triggers for seizures and whether there is anything that should be avoided at school. On this note, it is important to know whether I have photosensitive Epilepsy so that my teacher can be aware if flickering lights are a trigger for me.

- It is important that the relevant educational support agency has spent time observing me in the classroom. Following this, they will be able to talk with both my class teacher and my parents/carers to advise and negotiate useful strategies for my education. Being observed in class by someone other than my teacher may be useful in seeing the bigger picture.

- Books which explain Epilepsy are an excellent resource to have in the classroom to educate other children and staff within the school. Understanding and educating others can have an enormous effect on my ability to 'fit in' and on creating positive relationships with my peers.

- Everyone in school who I come into contact with should know about my condition and how it affects me. This should be supported with an action plan[1] which has been created specifically for me. It will allow everyone to act confidently and responsibly should they be around me at the time of a seizure, as well as know any accommodations that have been made for me. A picture of me on the staffroom notice board along with my action plan is vital.

- Often parents/carers go through stages of stress when their children are diagnosed with Epilepsy. My teacher can help by understanding that my parents/carers may feel worried about my safety at school or my education and as a result may need plenty of reassurance. They may appear frustrated by my experiences in school. Sometimes these feelings may be directed at the teacher. Try to empathise with the point of view of my parents/carers and try not to feel at fault. Plenty of communication will help to reassure my parents/carers that everyone is working in my best interests."

---

1   The terminology for this may vary from country to country – for example, a School Action Plan in the UK or a 504 Plan in the US.

UNDERSTANDING MY FEELINGS

- "My Epilepsy may create periods of instability in my school life if I need to attend medical appointments, undergo testing or begin taking/changing medication. These times may lead to changes in my behaviour or cause periods of absence, which may make me feel unsettled at school.

- Because of my seizures, sometimes the world can feel discontinuous, unpredictable and daunting. This can affect my confidence and self-esteem. It is important that I am made to feel safe and supported, particularly at school.

- If my seizures happen at school, I can sometimes feel embarrassed. Comments from other children may affect my self-esteem or make me feel isolated. It may help me if my teacher ensures that other children are educated about my condition. It may also help if I am allocated a responsible older child to act as a 'buddy'.

A few adjustments and considerations to the way in which I am supported at school can have a major impact on my enjoyment of school life and my ability to progress. Please do not underestimate the positive effect my teacher's actions can have. Thank you!"

Recommended reading, organisations and websites

If you would like to find out more about Epilepsy, here are some useful books, organisations and websites.

BOOKS FOR YOUNGER READERS

Lambert, K. (2011) *Sarah Jayne has staring moments.* Purchase the book at www.sjstaringmoments.com. Sarah Jayne Possembury is seven years old and has "staring moments", a condition better known as Absence Seizures. As with any debilitating condition, the book shows us that, through simple communication and understanding, children can be empowered to overcome the obstacles they face.

Rocheford, D.M. (2009) *Mommy, I Feel Funny! A Child's Experience with Epilepsy.* Deadwood, OR: Wyatt-MacKenzie Publishing. Based on a true story, *Mommy, I Feel Funny!* introduces the reader to Nel, a little girl who is diagnosed with Epilepsy.

Lears, L. (2002) *Becky the Brave: A Story about Epilepsy.* Morton Grove, IL: Albert Whitman and Company. *Becky the Brave* is a well-written tale about a young girl's struggles with Epilepsy.

BOOKS FOR OLDER READERS

Skead, R. and Simmel, M. (2011) *Mighty Mike Bounces Back: A Boy's Life with Epilepsy.* Washington, DC: Magination Press.

Mike has Epilepsy. He worries about having seizures at school and being different from his friends. But when he starts playing basketball, Mike uncovers a positive way to calm his mind, improve his health and bounce back from adversity.

Kutscher, M.L. (2006) *Children with Seizures: A Guide for Parents, Teachers, and Other Professionals.* London: Jessica Kingsley Publishers.

This concise, accessible handbook for families, friends and carers of children with seizures provides all the information they need to approach seizures from a position of strength.

Gay, K. (2007) *Epilepsy: The Ultimate Teen Guide (It Happened to Me).* Lanham, MD: Scarecrow Press.

Teens can lead normal, active lives despite having Epilepsy, and this book shows them how other teens are doing so.

ORGANISATIONS AND WEBSITES

UK

Epilepsy Society
Chesham Lane
Chalfont St Peter
Buckinghamshire
SL9 0RJ
www.epilepsysociety.org.uk
Phone: +44 (0)1494 601 300

Young Epilepsy
St Piers Lane
Lingfield
Surrey
RH7 6PW
www.youngepilepsy.org.uk
Email: info@youngepilepsy.org.uk
Phone: +44 (0)1342 832243

Epilepsy Action
New Anstey House
Gate Way Drive
Yeadon
Leeds LS19 7XY
www.epilepsy.org.uk
Email: epilepsy@epilepsy.org.uk
Phone: +44 (0)113 210 8800

UK Epilepsy Blog
www.ukepilepsy.com
The UK Epilepsy Blog offers support, advice, stories, shares
experiences about Epilepsy and also provides news about Epilepsy
and seizures.

BBC Health
www.bbc.co.uk/health/epilepsy
A UK website with information on Epilepsy and local resources for
UK residents living with Epilepsy.

USA

Epilepsy Foundation
8301 Professional Place
Landover, MD 20785-7223
www.epilepsyfoundation.org
Email: ContactUs@efa.org
Phone: 1-800-332-1000

Epilepsy Therapy Project
PO Box 742
Middlesburg, VA 20118
www.epilepsy.com
www.epilepsy.com/epilepsy_therapy_project
Email: info@epilepsytherapy.org
Phone: 001 540-687-8066

American Epilepsy Outreach Foundation
www.epilepsyoutreach.org
The Foundation's mission is to raise the public's awareness of
Epilepsy through advocacy and education, as well as provide
support for those living with Epilepsy and their families.

Canada

Epilepsy Canada
www.epilepsy.ca
The website for Epilepsy Canada, featuring information on
Canadian resources as well as general facts. Also includes "Kids'
Corner" with reassuring explanations for children.

Australia

Epilepsy Australia Ltd
Denise Chapman, EO
PO Box 1049
Baulkham Hills NSW 1755
www.epilepsyaustralia.net
Email: DChapman@epilepsyaustralia.net
Phone: +61 2 9674 9966

Epilepsy Action Australia
GPO Box 9878
in your capital city
www.epilepsy.org.au
Email: epilepsy@epilepsy.org.au
Phone: 1300 37 45 37

Epilepsy Action Australia
www.epilepsy.org.au
A growing site with information offered separately for adults, children and teens. Good general information for everyone and offers many services for people in Australia.

International
Epilepsy Advocate
www.epilepsyadvocate.com
Epilepsy Advocate is a community of people whose lives are directly affected by Epilepsy, including those living with Epilepsy, their caregivers, family and friends. These remarkable individuals share their experiences with the hope of inspiring others.

Finding A Cure for Epilepsy and Seizures (FACES)
www.nyufaces.org
FACES is an Epilepsy organisation that funds Epilepsy research, education and awareness, and community building events for people with Epilepsy.

Growing Up With Epilepsy
http://library.thinkquest.org/J001619
"Growing Up with Epilepsy" is a ThinkQuest website created by two young, gifted students with their teacher as their coach.